THE GEARHEAD'S GUIDE TO ATVs

BY LISA J. AMSTUTZ

CAPSTONE PRESS
a capstone imprint

Published by Spark, an imprint of Capstone
1710 Roe Crest Drive, North Mankato, Minnesota 56003
capstonepub.com

Copyright © 2023 by Capstone. All rights reserved. No part of this publication may be reproduced in whole or in part, or stored in a retrieval system, or transmitted in any form or by any means, electronic, mechanical, photocopying, recording, or otherwise, without written permission of the publisher.

Library of Congress Cataloging-in-Publication Data
Names: Amstutz, Lisa J., author.
Title: The gearhead's guide to ATVs / by Lisa J. Amstutz.
Description: North Mankato, Minnesota : Spark, an imprint of Capstone, [2023] | Series: Gearhead guides | Includes bibliographical references.| Audience: Ages 9–11. | Audience: Grades 4–6. | Summary: "ATVs tackle the toughest land around. But there are lots of ways to make these vehicles faster and cooler and readers will love finding out how! Packed with action-filled photos and easy-to-read text, this high-interest book puts the reader in the driver's seat!"—Provided by publisher.
Identifiers: LCCN 2021059298 (print) | LCCN 2021059299 (ebook) | ISBN 9781666356649 (hardcover) | ISBN 9781666356656 (pdf) | ISBN 9781666356670 (kindle edition)
Subjects: LCSH: All terrain vehicles—Juvenile literature.
Classification: LCC TL235.6 .A54 2023 (print) | LCC TL235.6 (ebook) | DDC 629.28/7042—dc23/eng/20220124
LC record available at https://lccn.loc.gov/2021059298
LC ebook record available at https://lccn.loc.gov/2021059299

Editorial Credits
Editor: Erika L. Shores; Designer: Heidi Thompson; Media Researchers: Jo Miller and Pam Mitsakos; Production Specialist: Tori Abraham

Image Credits
Alamy: Amelia Martin, 8, Janet Griffin-Scott, 26; Getty Images: Jose Azel, 11; Science Source: Transtock, 29; Shutterstock: Aggie 11, throughout, design element, Artur Didyk, Cover, 13, Bilanol, 14, breakermaximus, 21, 24, diy13, 17, FabrikaSimf, 19, FOTOGRIN, 5, i3alda, Cover, luckyraccoon, 16, Maciej Kopaniecki, 6, 7, nikkytok, 15, Ruslan Malysh, 25, Sergei Domashenko, 9, 27, sirtravelalot, 23, 28, trek6500, 18, Vershinin89, 20

All internet sites appearing in back matter were available and accurate when this book was sent to press.

Capstone thanks Kevin Dick, technology education instructor in Mankato, MN, for his assistance in reviewing this book.

Table of Contents

READY, SET, RIDE! 4

BUILT FOR SPEED 6

GET TOUGH 14

MAKE A SPLASH 20

    GLOSSARY 30

    READ MORE 31

    INTERNET SITES 31

    INDEX 32

    ABOUT THE AUTHOR 32

Words in **bold** are in the glossary.

Ready, Set, Ride!

Vroom! An engine **revs**. And it's off! An ATV can handle almost any **terrain**. Its large tires grip mud, snow, and branches. ATVs are fun to ride.

Many people like to **modify** their ATVs. They add **custom** parts. They use simple hacks to make their ride even better.

FACT
ATV stands for all-terrain vehicle. These vehicles are also called quads.

Built for Speed

Sport quads are built for speed. They sit low to the ground. They are light and strong. The fastest ones reach 80 miles per hour! But you can make any ATV faster. Just try a few of these tricks.

An engine needs clean air to run at top speed. A clean filter lets more air reach and mix with **fuel**. This helps your engine run better. That means more speed.

High-octane fuel burns cleaner than other kinds. It helps your engine run better too.

FACT

Safety first! Always wear a helmet and goggles when riding an ATV. It is best to wear long sleeves and long pants. Gloves and boots will protect your hands and feet.

Wheels also affect an ATV's speed. **Stock** rims work well most of the time. But **aluminum** rims are lighter and faster.

You'll need to decide which type of tire fits your needs. To increase top speed, choose larger tires. On the other hand, smaller tires can **accelerate** faster.

Rough trails are hard on hands and arms. A better set of grips can help. Choose grips with a waffle or **tread** pattern. They help **absorb** bumps. They keep your hands and arms from tiring out.

Do your feet slip off the foot pegs in rain or mud? Try adding a pair of nerf bars. These webbed frames protect your feet.

Get Tough

You're heading to rugged trails.

You want your ATV to be in top form.

Try these tips.

disc brake

1 On steep slopes, you need braking power. Most new brakes work well. But if you have drum brakes, you may want to swap them out. Disc brakes are less likely to overheat.

Stock quad tires have big grooves. Their rubber treads grip mud and gravel. But maybe you're headed to super tough terrain. Then you may want to upgrade. Off-road tires have extra thick rubber. They have deep treads. They can handle almost anything.

If your ride is too rough, check your shocks. Maybe your ATV has standard shocks. Then you may want to upgrade to fully adjustable ones. Tweak them to fit your size and weight. They will make your ride smoother. They will give you better control.

shock

FACT
The first ATV was called a Jiger. It had six wheels and could drive on land or in water.

19

Make a Splash

Want to really make a splash?

Spiff up your ATV with some add-ons.

Vinyl wraps can change the look of your quad. They cover the body like a skin. Wraps come in many colors. Some have camo patterns. Wraps look great. They help protect your paint job too.

You're out riding the trails. The only thing missing is some tunes. Problem solved! Just add a sound bar. It can stream music from your phone.

A whip light or flag adds style and safety. They stick up in the air. They help make your quad easier to spot.

FACT
The Baja 1000 is a famous ATV race. This relay race covers nearly 1,000 miles.

A light bar can add some flash. LED lights look cool. They make your ATV safer too. Lights help you see better when it is dark or rainy. They also help other drivers to see you.

Tired of mud splatter? Add a windshield to your ATV. It will also keep bugs away.

You might even want to add custom seats or seat covers. They make your ride softer. They come in many colors and patterns.

You don't have to spend a lot of money to take your ATV up a level. Buy or make some **decals**. Choose a design you like. Put these stickers on your quad or helmet.

Now you've got the coolest ride in town. Ready? Start your engines. And . . . go!

Glossary

absorb (ab-ZORB)—to take in or soak up

accelerate (ak-SEL-uh-rayt)—to speed up

aluminum (uh-LOO-muh-nuhm)—a lightweight metal

decal (DEE-kal)—a design printed on a sticker

custom (KUHS-tuhm)—made to order

fuel (FYOOL)—anything that is burned as a source of energy

modify (MOD-uh-fy)—to change in some way

rev (REV)—to increase the speed of an engine

stock (STOK)—the parts of a vehicle installed by the factory

terrain (tuh-RAYN)—land or ground

tread (TRED)—the pattern of raised lines on a tire or other object

Read More

London, Martha. *ATVs*. Minnetonka, MN: Kaleidoscope Pub. Inc., 2019.

Marx, Mandy R. *ATVs*. North Mankato, MN: Capstone Press, 2019.

Shaffer, Lindsay. *ATVs*. Minneapolis: Bellwether Media, Inc., 2019.

Internet Sites

10 ATV Riding Techniques for Beginners
motosport.com/blog/10-atv-riding-techniques-for-beginners

ATV MX National Championship
atvmotocross.com/page/series-profile

Basic ATV Riding Techniques
atv.com/products/basic-atv-riding-

Index

Baja 1000, 23
brakes, 15

decals, 28

engines, 4, 8, 29

fuel, 8

grips, 12

helmets, 9, 28

Jiger, 19

light bars, 24

nerf bars, 12

seats, 27
shocks, 18
sound bars, 22
speed, 6, 8, 10

tires, 4, 10, 16

whip lights, 22
windshields, 26
wraps, 21

About the Author

Lisa J. Amstutz is the author of more than 150 books for children. She enjoys reading and writing about science and technology. Lisa lives on a small farm in Ohio with her family.